GEOR(

BURN MY HEART IN WET SAND

Troubador Publishing Ltd.
9 De Montfort Mews
Leicester LE1 7FW, UK
Tel: +44 116 255 9311
Email: books@troubador.co.uk

ISBN 1-904744-53-2

www.troubador.co.uk/transference

Contents

Introduction

Something of Whitman has snuck into Wallace – that same marrowy vigour, the uninhibited reach, that headlong urgency riding the surf-crest of its own abundance – except that, with Wallace, his narrative shirt-buttons are all undone. Here is thoughtfulness and tenderness in a flapping, non-linear world. Here is the gutsy inventor, up half the night hammering out his word-proliferations to just the right side of prolix, brimming his associative word-capacitors with unconscious charges and beneficent volts. These repetitive discursions sink determined taproots into wry, evasive soil; the poems bloom and frolic even as they disturb – even as they snuff, again and again, at the membranes separating waking experience from its unwoken representations. Unlike nightmares (or saccharine dreams for that matter) you never quite know where the noon-dreaming Wallace will end up. So, just sit forward and enjoy the up-ending journeys.

To an English ear, and at his best, Wallace refreshes like a retuned piano. If he sometimes seems hit-or-miss, that is all part and parcel of the extended tick / tock of his characteristically long-lined attempts to make the writing's very vividness and invention its system of navigation as well as its means of propulsion. He accommodates apparent unevenness as purposefully as the improvising jazz-player absorbs musical deceits and temporary infelicities. More often, the poems swallow their own stitched-in tails, disappear with an unexpected pop! to stop us in our tracks.

In the end, Wallace lets language do the talking. His approach, at once familiarly American yet distinctively universal, moves towards a register that is both warm and original, allowing poetry to find a way of speaking which (to modify a thought from Clive James) "keeps our eyes open to unconscious worlds – or should I say unconscious words? – precisely when everyone else is flinching."

Mario Petrucci

Grateful appreciation to the following publications in which some of these poems have appeared: *poetz.com*, for 'My Fixed Idea of You', 'Night', 'Suppose'; and *Loving Touch*, for 'Dog Is'.

Burn My Heart in Wet Sand

In the dream state we are what we are without having to actively 'construct or define' ourselves in conventional terms. Did you ever have a dream when you were without a particular age, experience, mentality, haircut – or when those circumstances shift or alter without need of explanation?

We really aren't aware – in a fundamental sense – of our external circumstances when we're dreaming, so apparently basic and tangible in the ordinary day-to-day sense but more like ephemera and insubstantial or symbolic in the dream state. In that sense, it seems to me that when we dream we seem to be more purely ourselves – the whole set of circumstances we call life has evaporated away. There are no social conventions to subscribe to, no external expectations to which we have agreed or are compelled to adhere.

In life, permissions are oftentime granted through the exercise of various philosophies, religions and other practices. We catch glimpses of the unconscious, unconstrained moment. But in conscious life, actualization of our fundamental selves is frequently prohibited to us by the constraints of social convention, self-regulatory mechanics, the imposition of government or law.

The dream experience is evidence enough to me that there always has been, and always will be, a greater freedom of self – "the poet within" – to which we reach as creatures of spirit, prior to our entry into the social and conscious world.

There is no guilt or innocence in the fundamental unconscious state, only the experience of the self, unconstrained. It is only in the courtroom of the conscious world that judgments like that are imposed. In a sense, this is why I write poetry – in the courtroom of the conscious world, and the society which surrounds it, a good poem is witness in defense of the accused.

Hopefully the poems in this small collection are admissible evidence.

George Wallace
June 2004

In the Wheelhouse of a Croaking Field

in the wheelhouse of a croaking field
there were perfectly candid lilies in solemn rows

in the vertical fields of summer a farmer in a blue apron
turned impossible hay out of passing clouds

it was a country of clockwork lakes and politely colored birds
everywhere i looked trains were running on time

i could not stay there forever all the eligible men were dead
the women had eyes like headlights at a stalled railroad crossing

when it is rain frogs fall from the sky like bourgeois lies
it is terrible to be cupped in the palm of a neutral nation like that

did i mention the absentmindedness of snow?
in the autumn of my fifteenth year

i caught a train and i never looked back
i was headed for berlin

Fire Only Understands the Skin of the World

fire only understands the skin of the world and the plans men have made for it.
anyhow that's where fire gets its business done, like men, on surfaces.
sometimes a licking sound like desire or heat bones in me too.
other times i seek matrimony in marrow or brain matter.
for example tonight, there is a dark wood in the eyes of the world.
therefore i begin my journey like rain faliing at the edge of the forest.
like a cloud that wishes to return to the place where god hides.
even if that means in the thicket of splintered bones and deep ashes.
perhaps i will be a better man for it, even better than fire.
perhaps any man who attempts to see into the heart of things is better for it.
i know this: i have seen into the core of a world where there is no fire.
only the bursting sound of god in his orange blazing heaven.

Moon Among Apples

she is shaking the orchard of its green men

the pear is a yellow lantern in her hand
the belly of the plum a small mean child
but the apple is more than jesus to her
ripe as sin and ready for juicy plucking
the way she looks this way and that
when night breezes in among the trees
the way he looks down when he is jealous
oh the bitter spilling of new black seed
oh the idle moon cruising in star jelly
anyone can smell the bursting fragrance
of fleshed fruit in the wetsoil in the bark
in grass in moss in shattered bedrock
the best specimens of the season fall
so early to the ground, and so easily

She Was Only a Girl From the Mountains in a Mountain Town

she was only a girl from the mountains in a mountain town
but for love i wanted to give her the instruments of the world
a necklace that sparkles like an impassable river in spring
when the world runs quick as the river with chunks of snow in it
and mountain boulders still tumbling to the sea along with it
as for me all i wanted was a tree full of nuts to sleep under
and the fragrance of a woman's arms like cloves or oranges
to cling to like a blind man clings when he is in a bright forest
when winter is finally over and the birds have returned from exile
i confess, i knew nothing about the customs of my own country
though everyone knows everybody's business and tells it, of course
it was obvious after a time her relatives would discover our secret
and that eventually they would lift their hands up against me
how could they, a passionate people, despise the passion
that comes to exist between two normal young people?
yet they did, and i have come to this place of exile
and i search for words to sing when night comes
and i am alone with my thoughts and these strangers
i have stood in the town square there are many women
i have stood by the water pump there are many women
i have stood on the iron balcony at dusk when evening starts
and there are many women they have faces like statues
there are many women they are all the same age
there are many women their faces are impassive
they are europeans they have aristocratic manners
there is no one in this place who can replace her
in fact there is nothing habitable here for me at all
except for the jungle and the beautiful humidity
and so i am writing a letter again to you tonight
by candlelight, to explain how silence falls upon me
like a stone falling from a crack in the mountains
and explain that i can no longer stand it anymore
and that i want to come home and be forgiven

The Classrooms of Neufchatel

the teacher's instructions were simple and pretty
the boy listened politely and understood nothing
instead of a face he drew a green bicycle
instead of a tree he drew the golden wind
instead of a flower he drew seventeen canoes
and a man in each one of them wearing bright feathers
and all of them following a silver shadow
cast by english chandeliers across the planet
the teacher was intelligent and her lips were beautiful
in the classroom a terrarium with crickets and mice
and a clock on the wall that ticked very slowly
and a rack and a sink and twenty-eight chairs
instead of a pencil he held a green lizard
instead of a notebook he wrote on a log
instead of a house he drew a blue postman
who walked to the mailbox carrying a very white cane
in his other hand the postman held a long leash
at the end of the leash was a prancing fox
at the end of the fox was a windmill and vines
and a pathway surrounded by sunflowers and pinecones
three happy gods wandered around the garden with enormous faces
it may have been winter it may have been the creaking radiator
it may have been a message in the cracks in the ceiling
or the sun in the window drawing casual rainbows of light
but instead of a smokestack he drew a violin orchestra
instead of a factory he drew a yellow bus
instead of a sun and a cloud and a bird
he drew a rickshaw and a lamp and a bag
and a sad olympic athlete doing aimless calisthenics
in the rain on a field that was covered with thorns
at the end of the field was a man with a magic bottle
at the bottom of the bottle was a shipwreck and a cow
and a hurricane and a himalayan marching band
and a train in a valley with billowing smoke
oh! and a tibetan pony standing eagerly beside it
a pony that slept in the corner of the pasture
a pony that danced through nettles at night

he ran with all the other horses of tibet
he never ran alone he ran with the moon
the teacher's instructions were written in pollen
they were surely very simple they were written in chalk
but just at the moment she walked to the blackboard
he was looking out the window instead of at her
instead of the chalkboard he read from the sky
instead of his schoolbag he shouldered a melody
instead of his teacher he saw a green mermaid
a speargun a starfish a boulder a loon
a bowl of spaghetti a calico cat
a dragonfly in chains enormous flames
instead of erasers he saw a great seabird
and the wings of the bird lifting him up
and everyone in the school going with him
all of them, up! over the school over the rooftops
flying away! somewhere green and excellent and anyhow
way beyond the classrooms of neufchatel

My Fixed Idea of You

you were the knife i lost the jungle path deep green red as a blade spilled
on the highway which slices through a south american canvas

your bed when i shut my eyes i see you lying there naked like the morning
the sun walked in and you and i were still making love

is it so wrong to confess that?

flower of the agave milk pulp sapping out my wound my painted love you
were the tattoo which grows like scar tissue over dawn's eyes you were
pierced flesh you were the carpenter's nail

you were the hound's tooth which has worked its way into the blind heart
of the world

Night

night he drank from a new tincup
night he slept in the shadow
night his only starlight
night hidden in a pattern of leaves
the color of rain a cross of contradictions
night a loom of flowers night asphalt in his veins
night a blessing of cops the park unmolested
night dead men slept like two birds
night in a burning bush night a wreath of thin arms
night a song that is of no consequence
night a pillow of hairpins night the dawn turned
night an open hand of war widows
time wound tight through the mountains
night the recently violated
night the waning moon
night a great mystery of wide-open country
fresh strawberries a broad marble stairway
friends with enormous appetites
night the sleep eluding him
night nothing on its mind
night the odor of burnt asparagus
night the welcome mat of strangers
night the spattering of a ceiling fan
candy tiptoing on goat feet
planets changing their bandages
night like gas or trampled azaleas
escaping through an otherwise empty canyon

Suppose

suppose the book of the world is raw gold in the mind of an elephant in a cage in a zoo in europe or north america

or an african king who wanders the banks of the nile is the memory of a jungle cat with reflective eyes green as the sun on cumbrian hills

it is reasonable to suppose that crocodiles eat bony fish in a puddle in new york city that all along the modern boulevard hartebeest wade that the sandcliffs of northport are roseate it is reasonable to suppose in the foothills of kilamanjaro eternity is a lake of understanding filling up with water from white cascades of tien shan mountains

suppose that fact is fancy that mudhuts are schoolrooms that a rwenzori rainforest is a handful of diamonds pecked at by pigeons suppose that boys in schoolyards catch moths like bats that girls in perfectly engineered mirrors bathe by the waters of kerala in moonlight

sometimes this world is the red unborn skin of a star!

sometimes knowledge is an impenetrable jungle sometimes the wealth of nations is concealed in glass jars sometimes ambition is a barrier sometimes a word is the last poem in the blood of a people sometimes revelation is the textbook of leopards sometimes a dream can save the world from the acts of men

suppose a lake is a desert fed by snow capped waters suppose a winter cloud gathering over the eastern parkway is a suit of gray pavement

suppose innumerable pink flamingo suppose buddhas in bamiyan suppose clownfish feeding on a coral reef suppose the shadow of a shoe-bill stork is an african falcon (once i read about a falcon it drifted noiselessly over the steppes beyond karuma)

suppose rain falling in seattle turned into sunshine suppose sunshine was shade suppose shade was a calm wind which raced under the wing of an african falcon suppose an african falcon turned and turned in the sky inside your skull suppose blue sky was taino heaven it is reasonable to suppose it is reasonable to suppose – it is reasonable to suppose anything!

supposing twilight on the savanna was a magician's story? supposing the hearts of astronauts fed on majesty?

suppose an undiscovered green valley where the first woman in the world lives suppose she is singing a lullaby she learned from one of earth's lost satellites

it is reasonable to suppose a lullaby it is reasonable to suppose the rolling serengeti it is reasonable to suppose the warm originating sun

it is reasonable to suppose the birth of the first perfect library in the heart of the world

it is reasonable to suppose that as you read these words, earth's original voice is singing to you

In a Bee Flown Meadow

as if the sky would be blue again

see how the weather stalls in heaven
exacting revenge

you take this blue egg
you take that blue egg
you take this blue egg

and crack it on the edge of paradise

out of the open mouth of paradise
a bee flies out

open your eyes
you have wandered for weeks
and your cotton shirt has become wet

wildflowers are on fire with themselves

you are a meadow of bees
when it rains

The News

we spent the evening on the patio anticipating the green movement of the moon like a seal or time under ice after sleep and there was this small morning you woke up with me on the wrong side of paradise but like you said what did it matter we were skipping nickels across sun ra's eternal ocean

and you looked up at me with your green eyes and you said the entire day was already caught like a wriggling black eel and i was an eskimo with a spear in his left hand and could i just stand there a minute, netsuke-like, while you sketched me, so i did and you laughed and life was naked and fine and we were in love

then we were frozen in the doorway of the municipal law courts and some people were speaking out against the war and you said most of them were only wanting to be seen but even if that was the case and they were caught up in the spotlight the cause was a valid one and maybe we should too

and i stood there in the crowd imagining the crush of your lips on mine and your tongue which was always like marsh grass to me waving under a body of smooth water and that was the only justice i knew and i didn't understand a word and i was only trying to hear what you were saying and not them

and i never heard english spoken so harshly and all these paralytic jerks leaping over each other with their anger and their insight claiming to speak for the people and for all i know some of them may have been the people but they seemed to be there all of the time whatever the circumstances wanting to be the news

unlike you and me or i mean that's what i told myself for the longest time and i thought you thought so too

and if you want to know the truth i still believe it and cannot be dissuaded by distance or career or time – or by the fact that the last i read you were up for a judgeship in maryland or some other state

we were just two people in love and wanting to be nothing much more than ourselves

I Fell Asleep on a Beach in the Sand

i was alone i fell asleep on the beach in the sand
my head on a blanket beside a white collection of seashells
pink and white and a pillow crimped out of sun no larger than a child's hand
i had been watching a single sailboat in the bay
all day it sat still in the water unable to pick up a breeze
here on the beach the breeze was dry and low to the ground
the thud of warm air as it played against my hair and eyes
i could smell the breeze it was the smell of wind that was just becoming air
unlike the dull upholstered air which happens on a warm day
the kind of air that has been used too much, baked dead air
the kind you feel when an adult closes a car door and you are still inside it
that kind of air, and the hot shadow of a child's cheek against fabric
in this case the little windpuffs cooked out in the open were fresh and alive
laced with the odor of seaweed packed with the silicone strength of quartz
infused with the sweet mineral molecular life of salt spray
and all of it rocked into an undertone of waves speaking low against the
rockshore
i lay there awhile i could hear the waves' instructions through a blanket of air
i lay there awhile i could taste the serious sound in my mouth of pebbles
shifting
i do not know how long i lay there but when i opened my eyes again i was
alone on the beach
the little pile of seashells was with me, pink and white, as close to my face
as i remembered
the thin tinkling of the shells was with me, rattling foolishly with every
puff of wind
the tumbling microscopic sound of sand mountains the rolling innocence
of single grass seed
a stalk of yellow seagrass stuck like a flag a chunk of quartz rock standing
pat against the sun
a single sandcrab tapping his six-legged way toward his home, all that was
with me
also the dull crunch of someone's footsteps where was that coming from?
the pathway cut by men in beach grass begins was empty, no one in either
direction
on the narrow stretch of beach between uplands and bay nobody either
i was alone, it was the last day of summer, everybody had gone home
i listened again i heard it: the dull crunch of someone's footsteps

i picked my head up i looked in every direction i looked up at the sky
i looked out onto the bay the sailboat was still there
everything was okay nothing had changed
i was alone on the beach in the sun

The Obsidian Armies of Persia Perished

i have heard the blind musician walk among men
i have heard the liberation of honest work
in the tools of hard boned men smoking with laughter
in the creaking muscles of masons over traffic
i have heard isis sharply singing
we have carved this statue from the mountain
there were workers everywhere
prideful and with much energy
the sweat and the blue dust of marble yards
the drumbeat of the original mind
the precision of chisel and hammer
the voices of men and war
the song of wandering sages old with god
the echo of this footfall that morning
how he spread his hand across the wooden table
these fingers these hands were made by god
we were made to undo the ties of dawn
of death and the tyranny which binds us
i have seen him walking among plane trees
and silently among the beggars at the station
i have seen his dreams spread themselves out
like many men's dreams, like blankets over the world
i have seen him drink from the black dusty mouth of night
i have seen him enter the souk like a holy man
and the glacial cavernous disappearing lake
walking among men who dream their mother's face
walking among men trapped in the hair of night's wet cobwebs
i imagine all morning your own city obscured like that he said
i imagine the icy underground river always trickling
i imagine life like a wound bleeding from the mountainside
i imagine stonemasons chipping at night
i imagine the giant statuary face of a woman
and a sculptor standing unaware in his birth valley
his eyes like frogs on the plains of semiramis
his eyes like the sunlight in a goddess' eyes
his eyes like golden turrets on a goddess' crown
his eyes like the sea mist rising up over the harbor of athens
on the morning of the day which came before
the obsidian armies of persia perished

In this Corridor of Light

a pane of sunlight in a corridor a lot of light a patch of light not too much light
a pane of window glass clear glass not too much glass
glass you can see through a pane of

window glass you cannot see through
the wings of a black bird

a black bird which cannot fly through clear glass
a small black bird not too much of a bird
a black bird flying in the sunlight until death hits it

a black bird in a pane of glass in a corridor of light
now there is plenty of light now there is not a black bird

now there is the body of a small black creature in green grass
green grass is a not small thing the body of a creature which is not flying
is a small creature lying in green grass

a creature small enough to hold in your hand is a creature lying in green grass
a black bird which would peck your hand is a small thing
a creature which is a small thing is a patch of sunlight

in green grass which is not flying if i was able to if i was a small creature
if i was lying in green grass i would peck your hand
if i was a small creature if i was not able to peck your hand

i would lie in green grass if i was a small creature in a corridor of light
a lot of light which has been disabled

In the Boneyard of Your Dreams

i am a shipwright in the boneyard of your dreams
a shipwright's scroll in my left hand, partially unrolled
this metal plane held close as death in the other
against night's drift i read your secret name
and another word which weighs down my tongue
i want to say this is not my dream it is yours
there is something blue like the sky in it
somewhere between blood and the infinity of rain
my eyes are rain too and search you endlessly
because you are sleeping in a crucifix of failed light
i pass my hand over your face and closed eyelids
your skin is like good plank wood, very well seasoned
i examine the line of your cheekbone for rough surfaces
where to place my thumb? where to place my index finger?
this taste on my tongue is a cypher of desert water
your hair brushed back is the history of our lovemaking
wood lathes turning are a windmill to me now
white clouds piled in against the mediterranean
are my one salvation – and your dream, why
it is a green river teeming with crocodiles!
over the river i count seven ancient bridges
each one leads to a place neither of us has been

Three White Eggs

because a farmer by a hedgerow scratching a small scalp wound on the side of his head
is thinking about his wife dancing and the tractor won't start

and a fourteen year old boy named paul is sleeping
in the shade of a nearby pin oak tree and dreaming of paris and acorns

and paul is the son of the farmer but not of the farmer's wife
and the wind picks up and the farmer looks over at his son

and the leaves of the pin oak tree begin to shake

i have written a poem concerning a nest in the branches of that tree
containing three white eggs

In What You Think You Saw

in what you think you saw you saw nothing
in what you thought you heard you heard nothing

you were in love with what was not you in me
i was in love with everyone you believed i believed in

we were together a year we were pouring ourselves out
we were into and out of each other like the sound of water

we were pouring ourselves down the true arms of love
we fell into each other like the already dark night

we were a cold place we were diamond mines
we were dug out of each other like fat coal

we were a paradigm against the cold we were fog
we were each other's rain we were everything

it was the year we chose to be us for ourselves
it was the year we chose to be the eyes of each other

then out of the flat shovel which was your voice
i heard you say you loved someone else

someone who was not me someone sweet and real
i heard you say you were in too deep

we were together a year it was a good year
it was the year we were in and out of foggy heaven

Panama

i quit the lyceum i took a stoker's job
i was your glaring jungle bird
because of your patriotism i meant nothing
i was south american
i was an undocumented alien
i was looking good and my small fists
were crates of bananas
there was a bar
there was hot sun
i was a century deep in it
i was all booze i was empty catechism
i escaped the mad calendar
i avoided your eyes
i ate like a lizard i forgot you
i bathed in street water
when it rained
your silence was carnal
your lips were a canal
a mist a darkness a familiar smell
your hands haunted me
the walls of my hotel room circled all night
i sat white as linen with river bats
at tables and plates i said nothing
i smeared bread i spat beans
i drank blood i returned to you
i swallowed bad wine with your friends
i broke glass in the kitchen
i purchased memory it ran through my veins
it only made me sad
i had no hunger left in me
i was the fruit and rotten plumage
of your lost desire

Wednesday on the Farm

wednesday on the farm
there was a cow
and a housecat
and three hens
and a man named peter
there was a woman who lived there too
but she was peter's sister
and we needn't discuss that much
the cow did not need milking
but the chickens needed feeding
and the housecat needed putting out
and there was a glass in the sink under the tap in the front kitchen
which was always filling up with water
and wednesday on the farm
the woman of the house
who was peter's sister
was always emptying the glass out
and putting the glass down
and looking at her brother
and looking at that glass again
which had filled up with water
and picking it back up
and pouring it out
while she talked to herself
in a language that sounded
remarkably like danish
and wednesday on the farm
was the day the woman of the house
would pick up a piece of red cloth
and toss it back down again
toss it, like you might toss a dead cat –
right there on the countertop –
and she would look out the window in the direction of town
because wednesday on the farm
was the day the man from the feed store
was supposed to come around
only a lot of times he didn't come around

and when he didn't
the woman of thc house
would look at her brother peter, and say to him,
peter! in this language that sounded
remarkably like danish
peter! sometimes i get so
frustrated with you and your drinking
i want to put my hands
around this fucking farm
and i want to strangle the life
right out of it

Rain in Tucson

in another life i was the software in the eye of a mechanical hawk
more recently i have been sleeping late and dreaming far into the day
in my dream i am an actual bird hovering over the rooftops of tucson
i was born in cactus in a nest of matchsticks and dry straw
i live in the desert and i hunt jackrabbits in the sand
in my dream i am also a man in the streets of tucson
i meet another man he is carrying a tube of glue
you know the kind, it's white, there's a cow on it
i can't seem to hold anything together, he says
he has the look of the desert about him, his face resembles mine
his body is wrapped in a cloak of sand, his eyes are yesterday's campfire
i don't know what to say – it looks like rain, i tell him

it does look like rain
rain that is about to burst into flames

Claudine's Calendar

i am a poet on wednesday twinned to a crocodile
you are satan on thursday in a beach chair
you are napoleon on friday at war with the lion
on saturday i am the gates of judah
on sunday i am a ship's hull crushed by a meteor
our time fulminates under the sea
on sunday you are serious underground sun
on monday i am a horseman with fists in tangled reins
you are a sailing ship on tuesday with your mast touching the sky
on monday in the fabric of a roman war god i taste your blood
on tuesday you are claudine on the spanish balcony
i am a figbush on wednesday tethered to a kite
you are a night bird on thursday singing in the twilight of earth's last hour
on friday i am a groom, dawn casts its dice on me

it is saturday, the stars are all fizzled out
let the wedding proceed!

Dog Is

dog is limping and fetched from fog
in shadow of heaven dog is not blind
mouth crawling after hid rat is dog
squirrel and cat and foxhole to dig in

belly down in log or rotted fish is also dog
dog is paw tongue and horse chestnut
the prowl of old rowboats is dog leaping
a litter of dog is wet tail and all new ears

boulder to be hove summer tick to be yanked
on july mornings crooked as porch paint
on faltering rock short cuts steep dog sentinel
in tracking blood creek where hounds bay

especially when three mallards forget to fly
he who defines the surface of water is dog

On the Dark Other Side of It

i'm looking for
a small tear
in the fabric of
the bright flickering
black & white american
tv world where james
garner lives & also
a giant radioactive
1950s texas gila monster
which tipped over
an eighteen-wheeler on
tv & caught it on
fire because & it's only that
i've been thinking about this
quite a lot recently but
i'm looking for something
to crawl through
whether it is a
black buttonhole or
only some windy bit of
west texas depression
because when the sun is at
the top of the sky & it is so
hot, so hot around here that
you can practically see mexico
& about all anybody can hope for
in this bright flickering
black & white american tv world
is something cool to drink
that isn't poisonous, yes! i'm looking
for someplace dark & quite quiet
& even if it is located in hell
or straight through a hole
in the face of the sun
some place safe because
& as i tell you this son, my eyes
are filling up with sun but

anyhow like i say
these days i've really had
enough of all this traveling through
the bright flickering black & white
american tv world &
seeing nothing, just the same
mistakes made by a different set
of people, the same & i mean
why be selfish? well
all i'm saying is this, give me
a small hole one small
uneven unexpected thing
just a little tear in the sun's
bright underwear for the wind
& incidentally you & i to escape through
& why, that's exactly what
we'll do, we'll wiggle
through it to the other
side & we won't look back &
who knows, maybe your mother
or my mother or someone else's mother
could just sew that hole back
up again, right behind us & then
it can be just us & okay a giant radioactive
1950s texas gila monster which
tipped over an eighteen-wheeler &
caught it on fire & yes, i suppose
james garner, he can come too but
that's it, no one else, it'll be you & me
situated quite quiet & safely
on the dark other side of it

Things and Fruits

las cosas y los frutos - pablo de rokha

this song which will be sung when oil falls out of the sky
and words and things and fruits and the sun in caribbean
sugarcane fields when wagon carts are loaded up with
the black shoes of peasants when tin pots and itinerants
when wheeling men peddling medicine when hunger runs
from the little people instead of at them – the sky is not
the limit the sky is not the shadow of a terrible black bird –
when once again a magnificent ship of raw milk and pure
anchors itself in the smile of a single child this song
which will be sung this hurricane which will unloose
its hair this song with terrific speed and agility with its
suppleness when love becomes the main character
in a romance that has not yet been written this song
when oil falls out of the sky, this song which will be sung

A Matter of Protection

there was a little song sung by a mermaid who swam past a shore at the moment an artist from the south of france was lying there

it was a snail song it was full of stars and he had plenty of love in his heart (her mouth was a small coconut, her song was sour milk)

and he heard that song and he moved to paris to be nearer to the epicenter of where it was all happening – hey it was 1922!

and he kept his paintings in the hallway beside the kitchen in the apartment building which he was living in and he kept his drawings in a drawer in a pantry

and next to the drawings there was an opal case and inside the case was a revolver and the artist kept it hidden there and he kept it very clean and he kept it very secretly

because he wasn't an anarchist or anything it was only a matter of protection

and the concierge who lived down the hall quite naturally did not approve of such things and besides there was a well oiled thug who lived upstairs he sang operatically and well

and of course there were cockroaches and mosquitoes and unusual women but also dark men who kept coming and going at any time of night or day and one of them might have wished to steal a revolver like that

all day long he cleaned that revolver, you know, it was his only lover

and when he wasn't painting all night long or drawing (which is after all what artists from the south of france living in paris do) he was sleeping

and when he was sleeping quite frequently he was dreaming and when he dreamed he saw that mermaid and oh, she was lacquered like stars with sleep!

time went on and he saw that mermaid everywhere, asleep or awake he saw her in white fingertips and the hair of market girls he saw her in fat thumbs and the ears of statues

her eyes were black pearls!
her lips were sea cucumber!

the artist from the south of france wanted that mermaid so bad!

one day he took the revolver out of its case and he boarded a train in the gare du lyon and he carried it to rome and when he got there he shot up some roman ruins

and well, that scattered the cats! and the revolver was confiscated by the fascists

but we all know what happened next, the fascists lost the war and an american general got a'hold of that revolver and he brought it back to washington and he gave that revolver to eleanor roosevelt

and eleanor roosevelt gave that revolver to a woman who she loved passionately and secretly and well and a number of years after that

the woman who eleanor roosevelt loved passionately and secretly and well gave that revolver to a woman on hester street in new york city who she scarcely knew but who i am told resembled a mermaid

and that woman, i am told, swims through the streets of new york city to this day singing oceans and seas and she sings a surrealist song

because even in new york city dreams are populated like heaven with snails and mermaids and stars and things

and a person with love in their heart sometimes needs a revolver

it is only a matter of protection

In Her Room

in her room a fist full of bristling nettles
books opening up a path or a horizon
on the dressing table boxes of pastels
a packet of immaculate mints ripped open
time thrown everywhere like christmas wrapping
tissuepaper magazines jars with explanations written on them
like a rare dream or hairbrush i felt humor sweep the air
the earth spinning around in its sweetest condensation
i saw a purple butterfly between a buddha and a lamp
day rose like the pelt of a great south american cat
there were ribbons and shoes stuffed everywhere
even now when i close my eyes i feel her hands
they touch my face in a fever and then withdraw
they return to the shape of a pyramid
the one she built for us
on the swollen banks of a cryptic river
i remember that morning i turned to wave to her
goodbye mother! i cried
her hair was beautiful
her eyes shone like the sun on saturday
everywhere the perfect banking of airplane wings
my lips were pasted together
my words were silent
my throat was on fire
there was skywriting everywhere
there was only one word in the sky, shame!
shame for the unpunished child
who has stuck his fingers
into forbidden places

Earth is Horizon Heaven is Height

i am a cutout pilgrim boy. you are a cutout pilgrim girl. i am holding a cardboard blunderbuss and wearing a stovepipe hat and a shiny buckle is on it. you are wearing a white apron and have a white bonnet and one loose string is falling from it. i have been out hunting all day. you have been inside cooking all day. the world is orange and brown and black and white. our world has two dimensions. earth is horizon and heaven is height. my eyes are without distance. your eyes are without depth. i am free of doubt. you are beaming with unexamined gratitude. thank you mother. thank you father. thank you husband. thank you wife. thank you children. thank you relatives. thank you indians. thank you england. thank you powhatan and john winthrop. thank you pocahontas and ann hutchinson. thank you beasts of burden. thank you chickens. thank you eggs. thank you boulders thank you tree stumps. thank you mud root soil clod spade becket shovel adze axehandle sledgehead. thank you wooden spoon clay pitcher glass bowl shingled roof. thank you iron shoed hooves and metal sled runners. thank you curtains thank you curtain rods. thank you houseplants thank you pets. thank you housebuilders roadbuilders automobile builders. thank you coal diggers thank you crop dusters. thank you tomato pickers and lettuce loaders. thank you truck drivers shelf stockers checkout register ringers. thank you furniture makers. thank you computer programmers. thank you bank of america. thank you our father who art in washington. thank you jesus. thank you buddha. thank you herman hesse jean paul sartre flann o'brien martin buber. thank you paul bunyan john chapman luther burbank davey crockett. thank you god of eden. thank you god of the lion lying down with the lamb. thank you god of vengeance and forgiveness. thank you god of mutual seduction and pregnant wishes. thank you god of penetrative and non penetrative sex. thank you warner brothers. thank you jesus thank you jesus. thank you horn of plenty shelled autumnal vulva of the earth goddess.

Wheat

i'm headed for palermo with my head in a bucket of beer – i tell you boys beer is good for a man's spine – when a woman i might've made an impression on if i was a bit younger (you know the kind she's been around the corner more times than she cares to count) or maybe not

comes around the corner and she says why you're looking about as strong as an ox these days in a dialect which is neither elegant nor so musical as italian (maybe it was the ghost of an ox she said) quite a strange language and also considerably more ancient like

what HAVE you been eating she asks and my she is pretty as you please (which i should be delighted to have someone so fit and womanly for a traveling companion though i have gotten this far so far just fine alone) so i pull my head right out of that bucket of beer and i lift her off the ground bodily (which is to say

her right forearm is slung dangling around the back of my neck and her great generous hips are hugging my waist) across the wading river in the direction of the sun (and i smile at her and i say good morning madam and yes why of course) i've been eating

wheat, wheat, nothing but wheat, plenty of wheat

Fortresses and Flowers

if i was a gargoyle in a cavern of the world
if i was a rock in the hands of justice
and judges sat on parapets
and gravity was my witness
if we had not smoked
from the calumet of warriors
if the saints rose up on monday
to testify against the prosecution
if at the muddy crossroads
it rained serrated turnips
and all day tuesday
in the marble walls of government
the faces of angels
were carved by monks
from the southern mountains
if weapons were turned
to pumice or spring rice
if my fist was not a root
and the soil was not furious
if the north wind was a turret
spinning toujour toujour toujour
if horses were not chariots
and arrow points were not laced
with cloves and pepper
if the future had not died
and returned to us unclothed
to haunt the microbial dawn
if summer had not crowned
men of great strength
with the phantom of freedom
if autumn did not display
its unchained appetite
if winter was only
the original idea
of winter

o unscrupulous soldiers! o

madwoman in the stars!
it is march it is march
this is a poisonous melody
i cannot close my hands
around the world any more!

if your hands
were less cavernous
to each other
if the west was a song
sung by pilgrims
and the nation
sat on a balcony
watching the parade
of dancing children
if wednesday never happened
if thursday was a school of magic
if families gathered
downtown in the armory
like a gallery of new continents
where injustice is sleeping
to swap memories
of venus in the east
of the full moon overhead
if the fingers of the world
performed a peaceful minuet
if i could choke war
from the city gate
if the despair of boulevards
if the hour of long shadows
if the breath of miracles
racing through the capital city
if friday was a committee of aldermen
if saturday was a battleship
at rest in the harbor
visited by school children
to learn how far we had come
from our former ways

if sunday was a breezy avenue
of fortresses and flowers

The Teller of Fortunes

everyone in this town worships something
smoke from a broken pipe means unexpected love
smoke in the hall means the transformation of sinners
smoke from a gun means the validation of money
predictions do not generally make the weather
but there is another room you cannot see into
and the teller of fortunes knows who will thrive in it
and tonight is unlike last night and every night before that
somewhere in the city someone's god is always listening
all night !ong someone's god named work in corrective lenses
all night long someone's god named the mother of democracy
the teller of fortunes hears laughter behind many bedroom mirrors
the teller of fortunes hears knocking at the bent metal door
the teller of fortunes knows the hermit crab inside your brain
she lifts an egg to the blue ceiling and asks you to hold it
your future a hermit crab spinning songs under the boardwalk
your future a holy grail at the hotdog stand you should listen to
the teller of fortunes calls your future by its right name
the teller of fortunes says three small birds pecking at a rat
the teller of fortunes says a savior who lives in your eyes
a thought comes into her face and to her it is wonderful
the teller of fortunes says fear rides on a subway train
she says the word more sweetly than you ever imagined
an indelible blue mark you have painted on your forehead
i told you if she came here the cops would show up too, eventually

Your God is Love

a leaf stirring on a park bench an overturned flowerpot black soil spilling out a dove beating its wings wind rattling at the tavern door soot streaked like the face of a messenger at the upstairs window

your god a path by the river after midnight secret mortar in the wall the rough calculations of a mason a joiner a carpenter the unspoken prayer of a wetnurse the whistling of a nightwatchman under the moon

your god the joining of cobblestones where the path to the harbor bends a turk restringing a mandolin a cat blinking its copper eyes a button a pocket a constable's shirt

your god the angle of farmworkers in a field your god harvesting summer squash your god the sound of splashing in a coldwater sink your god a handrail all rusted with rain

your god the taste of white peppermint the pursing of a baby's lips a lion mounting its prey your god mate and sole companion the only sun ever to appear in the sky your god first passenger on the last ferry boat leaving a mediterranean island

a ladle a rainbarrel a line of buoys clanging in the channel a nest of baby sparrows your god a chimney brick in the mist the stroke of black ink on ricepaper your god the horsehair the brush the bamboo handle your god the crease in the last piece of ricepaper after all the students have departed

your god calligraphy appearing unexpectedly on the pavement your god in broad daylight sounding his own name as if you aren't even there your god hanging at the intersection like a traffic light your god moving like the cars moving faster and slower and even stopping sometimes

your god in evening's blue light your god in winter your god in the look that passes between two men with their heads bent over a chessboard when they look up at each other their wild hair their heavy shoulders their unexpected attachment to each other

your god when two men look straight up into the sky and see snowflakes falling

Without the Benefit of Men

some words were searching through the book of man
for the right way to express the way they felt
having been separated at birth from god and the angels

how sad it was! that they had to live
here on this big old earth so far from each other
living in the minds and mouths of men instead of with each other

they tried this kind of man they tried that kind of man
they tried many kinds of men until earth was covered with history
until earth was covered with men in their triumph and in their greed

it became obvious – no man the words found suited them
so after a long time they abandoned the idea of men altogether
and they threw the book of man into a fire

and all the words came together then
and they spread their arms out like tiny wings on a great big cross
and they watched the sparks fly to heaven

and they laughed and they sang their own song
without the benefit of men
and men were speechless creatures then

and heaven filled up with men's tears

so many tears it began to rain

A Rock

there is a rock in the center of a man's palm which he throws and throws again
inside the rock there is a woman he desires and possesses and now he must protect
and inside the heart of the woman he desires is the black soul of an unanticipated desert night
and inside the black soul of the unanticipated desert night is a cave no light has ever penetrated
and inside the cave no light has ever penetrated there is a ledge with a shallow bowl carved out of it
and inside the bowl with a shallow bowl carved out of it is a single drop of water no man has ever drunk from
and inside the drop of water no man has ever drunk from is the gleaming eye of a desert lion
and inside the gleaming eye of the desert lion are ten thousand things a desert lion has seen
including death and god and hope and europe and also the ghost of an unsettled nation
and blood and sand and the bones of a people who have been consumed with greed
and a man with a rock in the center of his palm who has wandered into the desert
to satisfy that greed, a man who cannot find his way back out of the desert

Bury My Heart in Wet Sand

after a wise man dies his disciples memorize the song
after a foolish man dies his neighbors throw a party
when a weak man dies thieves take a holiday
when a strong man dies alley dogs bite his children
after a joyful father dies his daughters wear fresh words
like a bright garland of cinnamon and orange flowers
when an angry father dies his sons put on their weapons
and they go out to wage war upon themselves
when a man who loved no one has died
heaven is filled with angry accusations
gods point their fingers at each other
while the people go about their business
after the death of a man who has loved too many
the people bury their hearts in wet sand –
then they go out into the world
and they look for the love in each other
for which he was always searching

Green Apples

how could he say no? no! not even to the mosquito
buried sweat deep in the beaded soil of his forearm
in sweat and hay dust and o the glistening armhairs!
honest fabric the bunched wool of his golden armpits

a handkerchief in his left hand the sun on the steppe
like the other men sitting in a circle they are lunching
on green apples, the peasant poet eating a green apple
too, gripped tightly in his right hand under a yellowing sun

stung with green appetite he sings a blood-ocean song
these swollen waves this russian wheat these strong veins
gazing without words without the hesitation of his father
who never once thought to cross this mothering sea of grain

a thin smile has spread across the horizon, see!
he has spied a group of small white clouds
they cobble up like a team of farmhorses in the sky

Lue

shorn like a cornstalk in a crowded sweet potato field
i lay under a sandalwood cross the ward of your abbey
i lay in your hospital falling like a star into the black
nursing well of your eyes, lupe! your hands were soldiers
in torn uniforms running everywhere your frown was
your grandfather as he rolled cigars in the marketplace
your mouth was the bite of rum on my tongue – you told me
i was weaker than you, too weak to listen, too much
in my own mind, now you listen! it was not fever i was in love
with you for precisely one night, and would have followed you
through a hurricane in the heat of august – i stood there under
streetlights, i waited too long for you, lupe, i was a street dog

Fly Away Girl

her eyes were shaved from a white cloud
her lips were flowers in a cut glass vase

she was married to a bird with black wings
they fished for oysters in barnaget bay

they roosted in a peartree fifteen years
his habits were peculiar, she would not change

in the sixteenth year the bird grew sullen
and he flew away to the coast of maine

all winter she waited all winter she listened
all winter her two hands lay in her lap

when spring returned she went down to the harbor
at the edge of the water she sang along

in the sad lost language of children and seabirds
she sang to herself a flyaway song

A Dream with Philip In It

morning tasted like freedom on the cobblestones of some european city
was it budapest? was it prague? no matter. the nationhood
of the student revolution, and hope, was our medallion, and a cigarette
shared like a pillow or a bale of hay was sufficient barricade against
the government and its armor. we always knew that one of those among
us was not one of us, but not who. until tonight. i woke from a dream,
my hair wet as loose straw in a barn after the horses have been awake
all night and nervous, and i knew – it was philip. 'i was a ghost' he said
in that odd way of his. cleared his throat and looking down his long nose,
his shoulders haunched in the perplexing manner of a cat. how could we
not have known it all along. 'of course!' i lied. philip looked up at me with
that innocent unquestioning gaze of his. of course! i always knew it of
him.

In a Silver Mirror

sky was busy rearranging its hair
the morning the train conductor was electrocuted

this reminds me of the time my sister josie
a child completely without reflection

stepped into a puddle of rain
while looking into a vacant shop window

always the innocent one!
i should, however, mention this –

unlike the unfortunate conductor,
josie still lives! from time to time

she calls from god knows where
"i'm on the road," she'll tell my wife

and ask if we can wire her
some money

Floating Over Heaven

an ambitious man in a golden dream drives a nail into the spiked earth in search of power

he strikes iron
he strikes water
he strikes oil

an educated man in an imaginary boat drills the cryptic skull of god in search of nobility

he strikes truth
he strikes righteousness
he strikes war

a passionate man with impossible hands snares the heart of a woman in search of communion

he strikes desire
he strikes jealousy
he strikes love

an ordinary man floating over heaven opens his eye to the invisible clouds in search of nothing

he strikes nothing
he possesses nothing
he owns peace

March of the Futurists

they were surely in search of
a comprehensive international mythology

anyhow the leader of the socialist
concrete aesthetic movement

dressed in a top hat and simple black cloak
rode an ostrich feather out of florence

when he arrived in three days
on the outskirts of rome

the via vecchia spoke in tongues
he had a wooden spoon in his lapel

everyone i have ever known
was among those who exited the cafe

their hands described an arch
of paint chips and molten bits of lead

all that morning long a new typography
rainbowed in his hair and head and willing back

One Afternoon in the Chelsea Hotel

a clock jumps into the lap of a russian dancer
and just hangs there
a skeleton perches on a white armchair
suspicion stirs its bones awake
from nose to slumbering tail
i am a french cat! declares the cat
in limpid twitching expectancy
and pounces tiger-like
on an imaginary wellworn bit of dust
time limps across the halting carpet collage
the chair jumps into an ocean of septic prayer
this place is neurotic! shouts the calendar
and i am the only denizen of the original cosmic dream!
the doorman drips worse than salvador dali
there are residuals littered everywhere
one afternoon in the lounge of the chelsea hotel
america's avante garde falls into a deep purulent sleep

Give Your Words a Cake Today

give your words a cake today, today is the birthday of words
let all the minutes and seconds of silent contemplation join hands
let us gather mentally around the big-mouth's party table

tell all the nouns and verbs wearing silver bracelets
tell that pair of gutterals in the corner lighting safety matches
time to ante up! here comes the birthday barge

the human race is draped in fresh blue crepe and admiration
tell all the vowels! let all the fricatives in on the news!
mother tongue has hung the hall with plenty of streamers

a raft of presents all wrapped up in pretty purple prose
and everywhere and everyone in the room calling for a speech
speech! speech! speech! praise for the birthday boy!

let us all hear the one horn blowing
let us all stuff his mouth with plenty of cake

I Didn't Say No

there was this place and it was in san francisco and i was thirty and the world was big and it was getting bigger
and there was all manner of men and women and they were living in all manner of places
and it was the only world around and it was big enough for me
and i walked into it with my eyes wide open and i traveled through it as much as i was able to
and i didn't have much of anything to worry about and i didn't have anything much in my pockets
and that was okay with me and san francisco was a very beautiful place
and san francisco was a very wild place
and the ocean and the sagebrush and the fog
and the amazing coastal range bathed in full afternoon sun

and some people were beautiful and some people were not
and some people made promises to each other and some people made no promises at all
and after all is said and done i was just one of them
and we were living that's all and we made some magic and we made some mistakes
and we made some adjustments and it was all really just okay
and we were fine with that and it was so terribly not important and at the same time so terribly important
and usually we were very happy and when we weren't we did something about it
and some people took advantage of that and it really didn't seem to matter if they did
and i was one of the people among all those people and anyhow like i say

i was thirty and i was in san francisco and there were a lot of things
and one time there was this one place and there was smoke in the room and i couldn't see so well
and i remember there was a long bar and some stools and some benches along a wall
and a mirror and some bottles and a bartender and a crowd
and there was this woman and she had this large body and wide shoulders
and she had a big face and i couldn't see her face properly and i had been

drinking an awful lot
and that night a lot of things that shouldn't have happened started to happen and something happened to me
and i should have been thinking and i should have kept walking and not gone into that place at all
but i was thirty and i was in san francisco and i didn't say no
and then instead of being big and getting bigger
the world started getting small

I Was Sorry I Was Late

i was sorry i was late
but the highway was enchanting
and i saw many beautiful things
in the slideshow of literary silence
three swans at pebblebrook
gliding downstream to the cataract of dawn
i slept on a riverbank and watched them
there was a revolution of frogspawn
a featherless bird climbed into my lap
there were creatures hatching everywhere
some went eggfirst and quivering
onto the crawling shore

i was late, i was sorry
a featherless child
put its head in my hands
i experienced rough translations
the sky shook with new wings
a family of strange beings
who were just then opening their eyes
were my sole companions

i was late, i was sorry!
you will get no apologies from me
someone called out to the driver
he insisted we stop for the night
the roadside inn was crowded
the hallway echoed with coughing
the rest of us could say nothing
one of the women wept openly
she was from a powerful race
woodcutters of the northern wilderness
she dreamed that mist clung to her hair
her hips were a tomb of feral things
all night we hung onto her words like fear
all night long we stood by her side
the crown of night felt woolen and wet between her thighs

in the morning she gave birth, it was a horrible thing
twin thieves ran scampering into the sun

i was sorry i was late
but i enjoyed what i saw
in the unspelled forest
a woman unloosed her blouse
a man put down his shield
a cloud gave birth to miracles
frost was gathering in the branches
we were detained for a week
the authorities were suspicious

i was sorry i was late i was sorry i was late
but there were inspectors
they were examining everything
they handled the children like grapefruit
they handled the men like fugitives
they handled the women like wolves
we were foreigners at the gate
we were detained for a year

i was sorry i was late
i was put into your infantry
i killed many for your country
i was not entirely unhappy
until the mud began singing
with the blood of my brothers

Rush Hour

morning is a treetop in your city hours before the real traffic begins
if we had a son together, you and i, we could name him rush hour
he would be the star of a movie and he would be beautiful like you
which would be helpful considering the kind of luck i've had recently

anyhow life is full of blessings especially when you least expect it
it would take a long time and all the birds in hollywood to explain
how the stars would sing our child awake on a morning like this
knowing how stubborn the earth can be when it's been sleeping

more stubborn than the sun in august with its fiery useless fists
more stubborn than truck tires beating down on last night's rain
more stubborn than the eyes of a catfish in a bottomless puddle
more stubborn than a morning that hasn't happened yet and besides

definitions don't mean much when it comes to love and first wishes
i hardly know you standing there a new woman in the independent sun
trying to break night up into wind or bread or quantifiable promises
words that can be placed into the mouths of fatherless children

crust for the pigeons i've seen you feeding down at the playground

A Rose is Every Gunshot

a rose is every gunshot
you can possibly see
on the thorny surface
of the living world

they are hunting
in heaven today
today in heaven
they are hunting war

it is open season
on fear and hate
in heaven today
hey, they are killing fear

in heaven that is
war is in heaven and
it is hell on war and
a rose is every gunshot

and in every row of cabbages
in the stinking sun in june
in a white dahlia flower too
every rose today is a gunshot

what a rhythm, a rhythm!
everywhere in the living world
even among the thorns
there is dancing today

on the surface of all the mud puddles of the world

you can hear what's happening
you can smell it in raindrops
you can taste it on the lips
of all the red roses

can you see it?
hey, can you see?
it is a really bad day
for war in heaven today!

a great rush of noise
across the face
of the living world
that's the wind!

and the wind is talking
because rain is bullets
and a rose is every gunshot
and anger and fear and hatred and war

they are all lined up today,
today they are all lined up
like refugees at a border crossing
how madly they are trying

they are trying like mad
anger and fear and hatred
and especially war, especially
war, all of them

trying to escape from heaven

American Sycamore

sometimes instead of your eyes i climb a ladder of birds

sometimes instead of your tide i peel back the bark of the world

sometimes instead of your lips i place a fingertip to the wind

to the east the moon is out; to the west the moon is out too

a horseshoe crab steers between two moons, how rare our love is!

we sit speechless under the shade of an enormous sycamore

a scroll of blue mist rises from the folds of centershore road

some day i will place the tip of my thumb against an orange sun

as it hums its way across still water in the direction of connecticut

and i will block it out

IN THE SAME SERIES

Published by *Ripostes*

Rip Bulkeley – *War Times*
Jeremy Hilton – *Slipstream*
Helen Kidd – *Ultraviolet Catastrophe*
Erminia Passannanti – *Mistici*
Ennio Abate – *Salernitudine*
Jill Haas – *The Last Days*
Brian Levison – *Adding an A*
Erminia Passannanti – *La realtà*

Published by *Troubador*

Anna Cole – *Out of the Matrix*

Larry Jaffe – *The Anguish of the Blacksmith's Forge*

Astremo/Ciofi/ Lucini/Passannanti – *Poesia del dissenso*

Francesco Agresti – *Itaca o dell'isola impossibile*

Erminia Passannanti – *Il Corpo & il Potere: Salò o le 120 giornate de Sodoma di Pier Paolo Pasolini*

Mario Moroni and John Butcher (eds)
From Eugenio Montale to Amelia Rosselli: Italian Poetry in the Sixties and Seventies

Printed in the United Kingdom
by Lightning Source UK Ltd.
101575UKS00001B/19-132

9 781904 744535